The Best Jokes from Boys' Life

About the Book

Several generations of boy readers collected these jokes and mailed them to BOYS' LIFE magazine in a monthly avalanche of postcards. These are their favorites, and each one may have been printed twice or two dozen times over fifty-odd years. There are straight man jokes, and slicker-vs-hick jokes. There are Boy Scout jokes, but not one about getting an old lady across the street. There are daffynitions (and no other word could define that type of joke better than 'daffynition'). And for the would be joke-teller, there are a few hints on how to milk the most laughs from a joke.

The Best Jokes From Boys' Life

Selected by the Editors of Boys' Life

G. P. Putnam's Sons

New York

Copyright © 1970 by Boy Scouts of America. By permission of *Boys' Life* magazine, owned and published by the Boy Scouts of America.

All rights reserved. Published simultaneously in Canada by Longmans Canada Limited, Toronto.

Library of Congress Catalog Card Number: 74–104392

PRINTED IN THE UNITED STATES OF AMERICA
SBN: GB 399-20014-2

Fourth Impression

Contents

Introduction: When Is a Joke a Joke 7

1 There's Always a Straight Man 9

2 Wheels 43

3 Two-legged and Four-legged Creatures 49

4 Hicks and Slickers 59

5 Play on Words 65

6 Daffynitions 81

7 Just for Laughs 87

INTRODUCTION

When Is a Joke a Joke?

A joke is not necessarily a joke because it is new or clever or timely, although any or all these factors can help. A joke is a joke if it gets laughs. Sometimes it is a joke when it gets groans. You can usually tell by the timbre of the groan whether there is appreciation lurking behind it.

Your grandfather may have laughed at some of the jokes in this book. Your father certainly did. But even an old joke can be funny if it isn't bungled by the joketeller.

One important point in telling a joke successfully is the punch line. It must be clear and brief and not too subtle. The punch line is your last chance to put the joke across. So do not try to memorize the entire joke. Memorize the punch line. You can improvise the first part of the joke when you know exactly the punch line you are building up to.

Another device for enhancing a joke is to make it appropriate to your company or the occasion. Change a name or an occupation or other reference when it fits the situation. For instance, if you know a good joke about a carpenter (but not just about carpentry) and you are telling it to a plumber or a plumber's son, change it to be about a plumber.

If you like the "straight man" category of jokes, you will find them to be more fun when they seem spontaneous. The straight man joke usually has three parts. For our purposes, we will call them the lead line, the straight line, and the punch line. Sometimes it may just begin with the straight line. Keep that in mind, for there may come a time when a friend will just out of the blue say something close to the straight line of a joke you know. Be alert, and adapt the punch line if necessary.

Sometimes you can set up a friend by paraphrasing the lead line in such a way that he almost has to respond with the straight line.

A joke is not funny if it merely offends someone or makes him appear ridiculous. A joke is only a joke when everybody laughs.

Chapter 1

There's Always a Straight Man

The phone rang at the firehouse just five minutes after the men had retired for their afternoon nap. "It's a terrible blaze at my house," the voice frantically cried. "The flames are licking through the basement and the first floor. Pretty soon they'll ravage the entire place."

"Did you try throwing water over it?" asked the fire chief.

"Yes."

"Then there's no use our coming. That's all we do."

JIM: *How did you get that black eye?*
MIKE: *I got hit by a guided muscle.*

JIM: *Did your wife lose much weight on her diet of coconuts and bananas?*
JOHN: *Only a couple of pounds, but you should see her climb a tree!*

JOE: Which boat did the Pilgrims come on?
MOE: The *Mayflower*.
JOE: Which boat did the doctors come on?
MOE: The *Blood Vessel*.
JOE: Which boat did the midgets come on?
MOE: The *Shrimp Boat*.

SERGEANT: *So you're complaining of finding sand in your soup?*
PRIVATE: *Yes, sir.*
SERGEANT: *Did you join the Army to serve your country or to complain about the food?*
PRIVATE: *I joined the Army to serve my country, not to eat it.*

One day John came rushing in from school and went straight to his father and said, "Guess what someone said to me today."

"What, son?" replied the father.

"Someone said that I looked just like you," he answered.

Puffing his cigar proudly, the father asked, "What did you say?"

"Nothing," said the son, "he was a big boy."

"There! I've got it flowing again. Now what was your name and address, please?"

TEACHER: *We know that the ruler of Russia was called the czar and his wife the czarina. Now, what were their children called?*
PUPIL: *Czardines.*

JACK: Look at that ugly thing on your neck.
JANE: Ah! What is it?
JACK: Your head.

JOE: What goes ninety-nine thump, ninety-nine thump?
MOE: I don't know. What?
JOE: A centipede with a wooden leg.

A mechanic was working on a car in the garage when a man came in with a small dog. While the men were talking, the dog started to lick up some gasoline from a pan on the floor. Suddenly, the dog tore out of the garage and ran about a half mile down the road, stopped, and just rolled.

When the two men reached him, the owner said, "Is he dead?"

The mechanic answered, "No, he just ran out of gas!"

MOTORIST: I've killed your cat, but I've come to replace it.
LADY: Very well, but do you think you can catch mice?

PATIENT: *Doctor, I'm having trouble with my memory. I can't remember a thing.*
DOCTOR: *How long have you had this condition?*
PATIENT: *How long have I had what condition?*

PHIL: Boy, today is the big exam, and am I nervous! I even have butterflies in my stomach.
BILL: Why don't you take an aspirin?
PHIL: I did.
BILL: What happened?
PHIL: The butterflies started playing Ping-pong with it.

"Tommy," scolded his mother, "I wish you'd stop reaching for things at the table. Haven't you got a tongue?"

"Yes," he said, "but my arms are longer."

TEACHER: Billy, what are you doing? Learning something?
BILLY: No, Teacher, I'm listening to you.

MA: *Pa, I think it's time that we should think of our daughter getting married.*
PA: *Oh, let her wait until the right man comes along.*
MA: *Why wait? I didn't.*

A man got in an elevator and asked to be taken to the top floor. Being new at the job, the operator went slightly faster than he should. After they had stopped, he turned to the man and said, "Did I go too fast for you, sir?"

"Oh, no," replied the man. "I always wear my necktie around my hips."

A butcher in London put up a sign in his window: THE QUEEN BUYS HER MEAT HERE. *A rival butcher across the street put up a sign:* GOD SAVE THE QUEEN.

MARIE: Sometimes I think that my husband doesn't care for me anymore.
LUCY: Why do you say that?
MARIE: He hasn't come home for three years.

YOUNGSTER: *What did one octopus say to another?*
FRISTIE: *I don't know. What?*
YOUNGSTER: *One of these days, pow, pow, pow, pow, pow, pow, pow—right in the kisser.*

DICK: Pick up that trunk you dropped. Mr. Cross doesn't want it there.
NICK: Who is Mr. Cross?
DICK: The man under the trunk.

BOYFRIEND: *I'm not rich and don't have a yacht or convertible like Harry, but I love you, dear.*
GIRLFRIEND: *I love you, too, but tell me more about Harry.*

A teacher was taking her class through a tour of a museum, and they were quite noisy. Halting them, the teacher said, "I want it so quiet I can hear a pin drop!"

About a minute went by of absolute silence, and then one of the pupils piped up, "Well, let 'er drop."

An old river steamer making a historic trip had stopped because of the dense fog. An impatient passenger asked why they had stopped.

"Can't see up the river," the captain answered.

"But I can see stars overhead," replied the passenger.

"Yes," agreed the captain, "but unless the boilers explode, I don't intend to go that way."

While seated at an exclusive dinner party, a gentleman noticed that the man sitting on his right was putting cauliflower on top of his head. After a while, he could hold his curiosity no longer, and he whispered to the cauliflower-covered guest:

"Sir, why are you putting cauliflower on your head?"

"Oh, terribly sorry," said the man on the right, looking ashamed. "I thought it was spinach."

A little boy threw a tantrum in a drugstore. "My mama won't buy me a cap pistol!" he cried.

"Well, now," said the druggist, "does your mother always buy you what you want whenever you go into a tantrum?"

"No," replied the boy. "Sometimes she doesn't, but it isn't any trouble to scream."

HARRIS: Good morning, Coy. How's the weather?
COY: Arthur says it's twelve below.
HARRIS: Arthur who?
COY: Our thermometer.

SUSPICIOUS NEIGHBOR: Hello, Jones, what are you up to?
JONES: Burying my pet canary.
SUSPICIOUS NEIGHBOR: Look here! I happen to know that you're burying my cat.
JONES: You're quite right, old man, but my canary happens to be inside him.

The children were in the midst of a free-for-all when their father entered the room. "Dave," he demanded, "who started this?"

"Well," replied Dave, "it all started when Hank hit me back."

Then there's the man who took his huge great Dane to the veterinarian and said, "Doctor, you got to do something. My dog does nothing but chase sport cars."

"Well," replied the vet, "that's nothing; all dogs chase cars."

"Yes," the man agreed. "But mine catches them and buries them in the backyard."

Two cannibals, a mother and son, were stalking through the jungle one day. Suddenly there was a roar in the sky, and the child ran to his mother for protection. "It's all right. It's an airplane," said the mother.

"What's that?" asked the boy.

The mother replied, "It's a little like a lobster. There's an awful lot you have to throw away, but the insides are delicious."

Two teens met on the street. One of them was leading a bulldog on a leash. "Look what I got for my girlfriend," said one.

"Boy," was the reply, "how did you ever make a trade like that?"

At the beginning of the school year a teacher in the first grade asked a boy, "What is your name?"

"Julie," replied the boy.

"No," said the teacher. "You shouldn't use nicknames in school. Your name is Julius."

Turning to another boy in the class she asked the same question. He answered, "Billyus."

"You ought to be ashamed," a father told his lazy son. "When George Washington was your age, he was a surveyor."

"And when he was your age," the boy replied, "he was President of the United States."

In a bank a little boy suddenly called out at the top of his voice, "Did anyone drop a roll of bills with a rubber band around it?"

Several people at different teller's windows answered, "I did!"

"Well I just found the rubber band," said the boy.

JOE: *My girl wants me to get a job.*
SAM: *Yeah? What are you looking for?*
JOE: *A new girl.*

JIM: *Now my wife is trying to reduce. This morning she touched the floor without bending her knees.*
FRED: *How did she do that?*
JIM: *She fell out of bed.*

SON: Dad, what makes an elephant so big?
FATHER: I don't know, son.
SON: Why is a lion dangerous?
FATHER: I don't know, son.
SON: Am I bothering you with my questions?
FATHER: Not at all. You'll never learn anything if you don't ask.

ARTIST: *And now for my latest painting. I call it "Cow Eating Grass."*
BOY: *Where's the grass?*
ARTIST: *The cow ate it all.*
BOY: *Where's the cow?*
ARTIST: *Why should she hang around when the grass is gone?*

A Texan visiting New York City was looking up at the Empire State Building. A man passing by said to the Texan, "Some building, isn't it?"

"Sure is," said the Texan. "Too bad you didn't get to finish it."

LADY TO STOREKEEPER: *I sent my boy for five pounds of apples, but when I weighed the apples, there were only three pounds.*
STOREKEEPER: *Have you weighed your boy?*

TOM: What were Tarzan's last words?
DAVE: I don't know, what?
TOM: "Who greased the grapevine?"

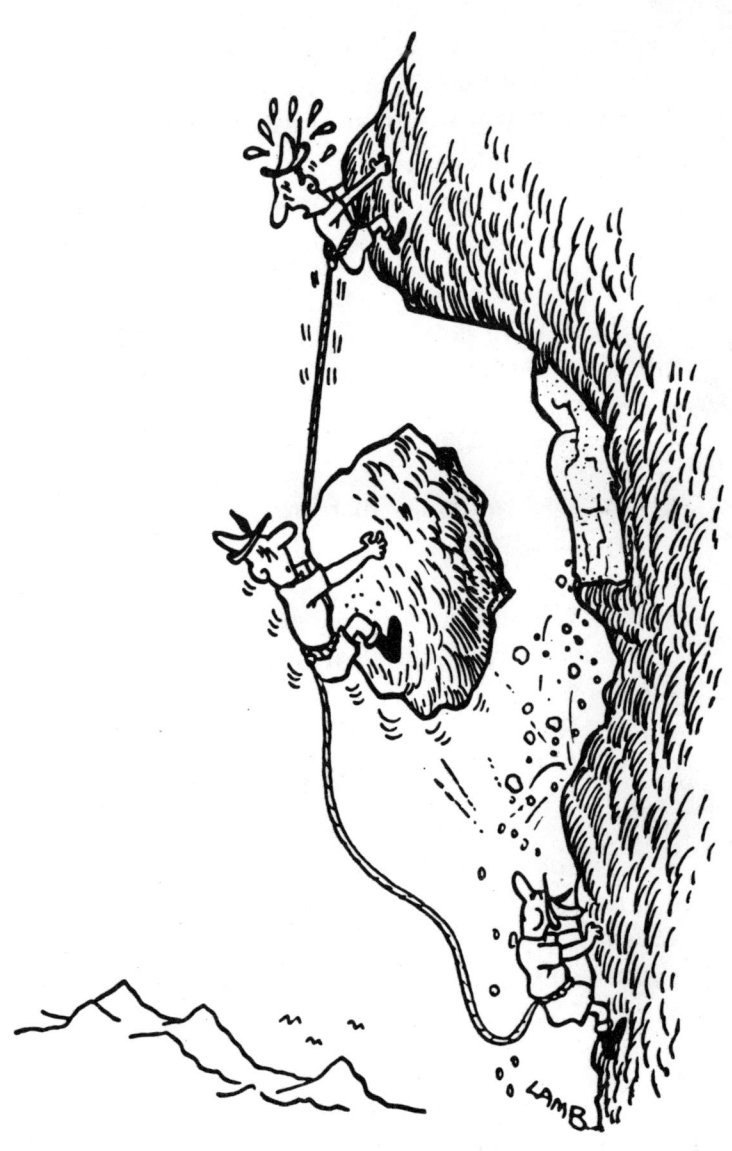

"Let go of it, you fool!"

The old lady was shocked at her grandson's use of slang. So she said, "There are just two words, Willie, that I wish you would stop using. One is 'swell,' and the other is 'lousy.'"

"OK," answered Willie, "what are they?"

DOCTOR: *Carrots are good for your eyes.*
PATIENT: *Why do you say that?*
DOCTOR: *Did you ever see a rabbit wearing a pair of glasses?*

LARRY: Did you know that bread is the mother of the airplane?
HARRY: No, I didn't.
LARRY: The airplane is an invention. Right? And bread is a necessity. Right? Now necessity is the mother of invention. Right?
HARRY: Right!
LARRY: So bread is the mother of the airplane.

X: I was named after Abe Lincoln.
Y: Then your name is Abraham?
X: Nope, I'm Charlie.
Y: But you just said you were named after Abe Lincoln.
X: Yes. Lincoln was named in 1808, and I was named in 1948.

CUSTOMER: Do you have alligator shoes?
CLERK: Yes, sir. What size does your alligator wear?

FRED: My teacher does good bird imitations.
TED: What kind of bird?
FRED: She watches me like a hawk.

BILL: When does eleven plus two equal one?
JILL: I don't know.
BILL: On a watch.

TEACHER: *Why is television an improvement over radio?*
STUDENT: *Not only can you hear the static, but you can see it, too!*

A policeman was talking to a beatnik on a scooter who was caught going down the wrong way on a one-way street.
OFFICER: Didn't you see the arrow, buddy?
BEATNIK: Like man, I didn't even see the Indian.

CUSTOMER: *Just look at this chicken you served me. One leg is longer than the other.*
WAITRESS: *Were you planning to eat the chicken or dance with it?*

TEACHER: Children, there will only be a half day of school this morning.
PUPILS: Whoopee! Hurray!
TEACHER: Silence. We'll have the other half this afternoon.

LITTLE JOHNNY TO MOTHER (*after his first day at school*): *I'm not going back!*
MOTHER: *Why not?*
JOHNNY: *I can't read, I can't write, and they won't let me talk. So what's the use?*

JIM: Doctor, I'm worried. I'm always blowing smoke rings.
DOCTOR: So what, quite a few smokers blow smoke rings.
JIM: But, Doctor, I don't smoke!

TEACHER: *Now see if you can understand what the word "sufficient" means. If I gave a cat a bowl of milk, that might not be sufficient. But if I gave a cat two bowls of milk, that should be sufficient. Now, James, what does the word mean?*
JAMES: *A cat full of milk.*

TED: (*while swimming*): I can keep my head above-water.
NED: Of course, wood floats.

DICK: *Have a peanut?*
DORIS: *No, thanks. They're fattening.*
DICK: *How do you know?*
DORIS: *Did you ever see a skinny elephant?*

JOE: What is jaywalking?
JACK: It is exercise that brings on a run-down feeling.

PHIL: *Why do elephants wear sunglasses?*
LIL: *I don't know. Why?*
PHIL: *Because there are so many elephant jokes, they don't want to be recognized.*

FIRST PYGMY: My father is four feet tall.
SECOND PYGMY: So what? My father is only three feet.
THIRD PYGMY: My father is in the hospital.
FIRST PYGMY: Why?
THIRD PYGMY: He fell off a ladder picking strawberries.

JOHN: *What word in the English language contains all the vowels?*
TIM: *Is there such a word?*
JOHN: *Unquestionably!*

CARPENTER: You hammer like lightning.
HELPER: You mean I'm fast?
CARPENTER: No, I mean you seldom strike the same place twice.

TEACHER: *Now children, we will have our arithmetic class. What would we have if you took twenty-four, divided by two, multiplied by six and added sixteen?*
GEORGE: *Er-um. The wrong answer.*

SON: Pop, will you give me ten cents for a poor man who's outside crying?
DAD: OK, son, here it is. What's he crying about?
SON: He's crying, "Fresh roasted peanuts, ten cents a bag."

ANGRY CUSTOMER IN A RESTAURANT: *Waiter, what's the fly doing in my soup?*
WAITER (*looking into the soup*): *The backstroke, I think.*

TOM: How do you spell blind pig?
JOE: B L I N D P I G.
TOM: No. B L N D P G. Blind pigs don't have eyes.

JOE: *What did one fisherman say to the other fisherman in the middle of the desert?*
MOE: *I don't know. What?*
JOE: *Long time no sea.*

TIM: How far can you go into a forest?
JIM: I don't know. How far?
TIM: Only halfway—after that you would be coming out.

DELL: *Why do elephants paint their toenails red?*
RICHARD: *I don't know.*
DELL: *So they can hide in a strawberry patch.*

JIM: *What did the flower say to the bee?*
TIM: *I don't know?*
JIM: *Quit bugging me.*

"Are you sure everybody learns to ski this way?"

A lady wanted to take her husband to a royal ball. Just to be sure he knew how to address the high people of the court, she asked, "How do you address a duke?"

"Your Lordship," was the reply.

"How do you address a duchess?"

"Your Ladyship."

"How do you address an admiral?"

"Your Battleship."

ZEKE: What's worse than raining cats and dogs?
BOB: I don't know.
ZEKE: Hailing taxis.

President Lincoln could tell a neat pun on occasion. The governor of a Middlewestern state was describing a small stream named Weeping Water.

"No doubt," suggested the President, "the Indians call it Minneboohoo."

"Why should they?" the governor asked.

"Well," answered Lincoln, "isn't it logical since they call Laughing Water the Minnehaha?"

SPIKE: *Our dog is just like one of the family.*
MIKE: *Really? Which one?*

MOTHER: What are you jumping up and down for, Paul?
PAUL: I took my medicine and forgot to shake the bottle.

JAY: I'm looking for a beautiful girl.
MAY: Well, here I am.
JAY: Swell, you can help me look.

NEWSBOY: *Extra. Extra. Read all about two men swindled!*
PASSERBY: *Give me one—Say, there's nothing about two men being swindled.*
NEWSBOY: *Extra. Extra. Three men swindled.*

"Are you a good little boy?"
"Nope, I'm the kind of a boy my ma doesn't want me to play with."

JOE: *Mr. and Mrs. Smith have seven daughters, and each of the seven daughters has a brother. How many people are in the family?*
MOE: *Sixteen?*
JOE: *No, ten!*

Two men were sitting in a blood donor station. One was an Eastern tourist, and the other was an Apache Indian. After staring for a few moments, the tourist could hold his curiosity no longer.
"Are you really a full-blooded Indian?" he asked.
"Well, no," the Apache answered thoughtfully, "I'm one pint short."

WIFE: *Darling, there's a mouse squeaking.*
HUSBAND: *Well, what do you want me to do? Oil it?*

TEACHER: *James, name two documents that have contributed heavily to our government.*
JAMES: *Forms 1040 and 1040A.*

JOE (*looking at Niagara Falls*): Got anything like that in Texas?
TEXAN: We got a plumber who could fix that leak in ten minutes.

TEACHER: *Eddie, your hands are very dirty. What would you say if I came to school with dirty hands?*
EDDIE: *I would be too polite to mention it.*

BOBBY: Mother, will you do my arithmetic for me?
MOTHER: No, Bob, it wouldn't be right.
BOBBY: Well, you could try.

DOC: *I've examined you thoroughly. All you need is a rest.*
WOMAN: *Why, Doctor, I need medicine. Look at my tongue.*
DOC: *That needs a rest, too.*

JONES: That music my boy is playing is very difficult.
SMITH: I wish it were impossible.

BILL: *My uncle drives a stagecoach without wheels.*
BOB: *What holds it up?*
BILL: *Bandits.*

ROSS: I didn't sleep so well last night.
KEVIN: Why, what happened?
ROSS: I plugged the electric blanket into the toaster by mistake and kept popping out of bed all night.

BOBBY: *What did the papa lightning bug say to the mama lightning bug?*
ROBBY: *I don't know. What?*
BOBBY: *Isn't Junior bright for his age?*

JIM: When they take your appendix out, it is an appendectomy; when they remove your tonsils from your throat, it is a tonsillectomy. What is it when you remove a growth from your head?
JOHN: I give up.
JIM: A haircut.

JOE: *Why do cows wear bells around their necks?*
MOE: *I don't know. Why?*
JOE: *Because their horns don't work.*

HENRY: Why did the Texan buy a dachshund?
LARRY: I don't know, why?
HARRY: Because he heard the other Texans saying, "Get a Long Little Doggie."

JACK: *What grows up while it grows down?*
JILL: *I don't know. What?*
JACK: *A baby duckling.*

HILL: What is the difference between a hill and a pill?
DAIL: I give up. What?
HILL: One is hard to get up, while the other is hard to get down.

JOE: *Why do you always find something in the last place you look?*
SAM: *I don't know.*
JOE: *You stop looking for it when you find it.*

SALES MANAGER: What's this big item on your expense account?
TRAVELING SALESMAN: Oh, that's my hotel bill.
SALES MANAGER: Well, don't buy any more hotels.

PATIENT: *Doctor, thank you so much. My pain is gone. What was my trouble, rheumatism?*
DOCTOR: *No. Your suspenders were twisted.*

LADY: My dear man, are you afraid of hard work?
TRAMP: Not at all, ma'am. In fact, ma'am, I'm on such good terms with hard work that I kin lay right down beside it and go to sleep.

FATHER: What are you studying in school?
KITTY: Mostly gozinta, Daddy.
FATHER: What is gozinta? A new language?
KITTY: No, Daddy, just gozinta. Two goes into four, four goes into eight, eight goes into sixteen. . . .

Lost on a back road in Alabama, a young man asked the way to Montgomery from an old farmer. The farmer looked down the road, scratched his head, and gave a complicated set of directions.

About thirty minutes later, after following the farmer's directions carefully, the young man could hardly believe his eyes when he came upon the farmer again at the very same spot. Thoroughly exasperated, he pulled up and shouted, "Look here, you act as though you expected to see me again. What's the big idea?"

"Waal, young feller," the farmer said, "I didn't aim to waste my time explaining how you get to Montgomery till I found out if you could follow simple directions."

FIRST WOMAN: *My husband is an efficiency expert.*
SECOND WOMAN: *What does an efficiency expert do?*
FIRST WOMAN: *Well, if we women did it, they'd call it nagging.*

"That new member of the student council seems to have a good opinion of himself," said the president.

"You're not fooling," agreed the secretary. "On his last birthday he sent his mother a letter of congratulations."

BOY: *When I start working, I want to start at the top.*
FATHER: *But, son, the only job in which you start at the top is digging ditches.*

TIM: *I found a horseshoe this morning.*
SIM: *You did! Do you know what that means?*
TIM: *Yes, it means some poor horse is running around in his stockinged feet.*

MATT: How'd you get that awful bump on your head?
PAT: Tomatoes.
MATT: Tomatoes! How could tomatoes raise a bump like that?
PAT: They were in a can!

One day a little girl ran into her house shouting, "Mommy, Mommy, the boy next door broke my doll."
"How did he break it?" asked her mother.
"I hit him over the head with it."

CLIENT: I'll give you a hundred dollars to do my worrying for me.
LAWYER: Where's the hundred?
CLIENT: That's your first worry.

TRAFFIC COP: *Lady, you were doing seventy miles an hour.*
WOMAN DRIVER: *Oh, isn't that wonderful! And I only learned how to drive yesterday.*

DICKIE: Why does a milkman use a white horse?
NICKIE: I don't know. Why?
DICKIE: To pull his wagon.

JOE: If a man walked into a café and ordered a cup of coffee and a doughnut, proceeded to dunk half the doughnut in the coffee, then eat it, then dunk the other half of the doughnut and eat that, how could you tell he was a sailor?
SAM: I don't know. How?
JOE: He was wearing a sailor's uniform!

WIFE (*at 1 A.M.*): *A fine time to come in. I want an explanation, and I want the truth.*
HUSBAND: *Make up your mind, dear. You can't have both.*

JOE: What are you looking for?
JACK: I lost a nickel. Did you find it?
JOE: No, but I found a penny.
JACK: Good. Give me the penny, and you can owe me the four cents.

CUSTOMER: *And this, I suppose, is one of those hideous caricatures you call modern art?*
ART DEALER: *No, it's just a mirror.*

HUSBAND: Well, I finally got the car fixed. Now it will start.
WIFE: How much did it cost?
HUSBAND: Only two dollars.
WIFE: That's not bad. What was wrong with it?
HUSBAND: It needed gas.

JOHN: *When I was sparring partner for the heavyweight champ, I gave him the biggest scare of his life.*
JIM: *You gave the champ a scare?*
JOHN: *Yes. He thought he'd killed me.*

JOB APPLICANT: Sir, do you have an opening in this office for a smart young man like me?
OFFICE MANAGER: Yes, we do, and please don't slam it on your way out.

FATHER: *Danny, why did you kick your little friend?*
DANNY: *I wanted him to go home.*
FATHER: *Why didn't you ask him to leave?*
DANNY: *That wouldn't be polite.*

CUSTOMER IN PET SHOP: I like this dog, but his legs are too short.
CLERK: Too short? Why, ma'am, they're all right. They reach clear to the floor.

EMPLOYER: *Why do you ask for a raise?*
EMPLOYEE: *Sir, I wouldn't ask for a raise, but somehow my kids found out that other families eat three times a day.*

JOE: A friend of mine crosses kangaroos with raccoons.
MOE: What's the idea?
JOE: He gets fur coats with pockets.

Jim had just received his diploma after four years of high school.

"I'm free," he shouted.

"That's nothing," said a little girl standing nearby. "I'm four."

A woman who was a great admirer of General Custer, hired an artist to paint a mural of what Custer's thoughts might have been at the Little Big Horn.

At the unveiling, the woman saw the mural for the first time. In it there was a cow with a halo, the devil, and peaceful Indians picking cotton.

Immediately the woman phoned the artist and demanded an explanation. His reply was simple:

"Holy cow. Where the devil did all those cotton-pickin' Indians come from?"

"How is it," said one dog owner to another, "that your dog knows all kinds of smart tricks, while I find it impossible to teach my dog anything?"

"Well, you see," said the other dog owner, "you've got to know more than the dog to start with."

"I sure wish I had my wife back," sighed the mountaineer.

"Where is she?" asked a friend.

"Sold her for a jug of apple cider."

"I reckon you're beginning to miss her."

"Nope. I'm thirsty again."

FATHER: *How do you get Mike up so early?*
MOTHER: *I just open the door and throw the cat on his bed.*
FATHER: *How does that waken him?*
MOTHER: *He sleeps with the dog.*

MRS. SMITH: But I thought you had an automatic dishwasher.
MRS. JONES: I have. But he's away at Scout camp right now.

TOM: *What are you making?*
RUSTY: *An invention.*
TOM: *Ha, ha, ha, ha.*
RUSTY: *Oh, they laughed at Edison, they laughed at Bell, and they laughed at Geck.*
TOM: *Who's Geck?*
RUSTY: *Haven't you heard of Charles Geck?*
TOM: *No, what did he invent?*
RUSTY: *Nothing, but they sure laughed at him.*

EDITH: I found fifty cents on the sidewalk in front of school.
EDDIE: I think it's mine. I dropped a half dollar there today and couldn't find it.
EDITH: But what I found was two quarters.
EDDIE: Then I'm sure it's mine. It probably broke when it hit the sidewalk.

TEXAN: *Where I come from we catch fish as big as eight inches.*
NEW YORKER: *So what. We catch fish as long as twenty-two inches.*
TEXAN: *I don't know about you, but in Texas we measure our fish between the eyes.*

The mess sergeant listened angrily to a complaint about the bread he served.

"I'll have you know if Napoleon had had that bread when he was crossing the Alps, he'd have eaten it with delight."

"Yes, sir," said the private, "but it was fresh then."

A pretty young lady went to cash a check at a bank. The teller examined it, then asked, "Can you identify yourself?"

Looking puzzled, the girl dipped into her handbag and pulled out a small mirror. She glanced into it for a moment, then smiled, "Yes, it's me all right."

CUSTOMER: Look at this new coat you sold me. It's split clear up the back.
SALESMAN: Why, that just shows how tightly the buttons were sewn on.

Her hair in curlers, a faded robe fluttering behind her, the lady rushed out and hailed the garbage truck.

"Yoo-hoo. Am I too late for the garbage?"

The driver yelled back, "No, ma'am. Jump right in."

DAD: Good heavens, get me a shovel quick! Georgie's stuck in the mud up to his shoelaces.
MOM: His shoelaces! Why doesn't he just walk out?
DAD: Stop arguing. He went in headfirst.

JIM: *What has two arms, two wings, two tails, three heads, and eight legs?*
TIM: *I don't know.*
JIM: *A man holding a chicken on a horse.*

Joshua Reynolds was a great artist, the art teacher told her students. "With a single stroke of a brush he could change a smiling face to a frowning one."

"That's nothing," said little Billy, "so can my Mom."

JACK: *Did I tell you the time I came face to face with a lion?*
JOAN: *No. What happened?*
JACK: *There I stood without a gun. The lion growled and crept closer, closer, closer ...*
JOAN: *Gosh! What did you do?*
JACK: *I moved on to the next cage.*

Chapter 2

Wheels

A bopster was speeding down the highway in his sports car. He stopped to help a farmer with a Model T who was stuck. He pulled the farmer out with a nylon cord and told the farmer to honk when the motor started. Off they went faster and faster. The bopster was going so fast that he could not hear the farmer honk. They sped through a small town, and a few moments later an officer phoned his chief and said that he was quitting.

"Why?" said the chief.

"Because," said the officer, "I just saw a sports car drive through here at a hundred miles per hour."

"That's nothing new," said the chief.

"Yes," said the officer, "but this one had a Model T Ford behind him honking to pass."

I have a car:
It never skids,
It never breaks down,
It never gets a puncture,
It never falters on steep grades,
It never gets in a collision or accident.
I wish I could get it started!

The motorist was filling in an accident report: "I was backing out of a parking space, and by the time I backed out far enough to see what was coming it already had!"

A railroad claim agent was teaching his wife to drive when the brakes suddenly failed on a steep downhill grade.
"I can't stop," she shrilled. "What'll I do?"
"Brace yourself," advised her husband, "and try to hit something cheap."

A young woman stalled her car at an intersection and after many tries suceeded only in flooding it. An impatient man behind her honked his horn steadily. Finally, she went back to him and said, "I don't seem to be able to start my car, but if you'll start it for me, I'll stay here and lean on your horn."

When a friend crumpled his new sports car, Bob said, philosophically, "Well, that's the way the Mercedes-Benz."

A motorist was driving through the country when his motor stopped. He got out of the car and raised the hood to locate the trouble. "The trouble is in the carburetor," a voice behind him said.

The motorist turned around, surprised, but saw only an old horse standing nearby. Not believing his ears, he asked, "Did you say something?"

"I said you'd better check your carburetor," replied the horse.

Rushing to the nearest farmhouse, the motorist excitedly told his experience to the old farmer. "Was it an old bay horse with one flop ear?" asked the farmer.

"Yes, yes, that's the one!"

"Well, don't pay any attention to him," the farmer scoffed. "He don't know anything about automobiles anyway."

A Texan was bragging to a dude about how he lets his son drive one of the family Cadillacs.

"But, Tex," replied the dude, "your son is only five years old."

"I know," said the Texan. "That's why I only let him drive it in the living room."

Two motorists stopped head on on a bridge too narrow for their cars to pass.

"I never back up for an idiot!" said one driver angrily.

"I always do," replied the other as he shifted into reverse.

BILL: *This car was rolling down the hill without a driver, but I jumped in and put on the emergency brake.*

PHIL: *I know, I was pushing it.*

A motorist, following a taillight in a dense fog, crashed into the car ahead of him when it stopped very fast. "Why didn't you let me know you were going to stop" he yelled. "Why should I?" came a voice. "I'm in my own garage."

Chapter 3

Two-legged and Four-legged Creatures

A salesman was driving down the road, and he struck a rabbit. He looked back and saw the rabbit flopping around in the road. He thought that this was unmerciful and that he should put the rabbit out of its misery. He was ready to kill the rabbit when another man drove up and told him to stop.

The second man took a little bottle out of his pocket and gave the rabbit a few drops of the liquid in the bottle. The rabbit jumped up and ran away across a field.

The salesman said, "That must be powerful medicine."

The other man said, "That's not medicine at all. That's hare restorer!"

Once a game warden was lecturing at a school. He was explaining that he used apples as bait to catch live rabbits. Just as he said this, a wise guy stood up and asked, "Why don't you use a picture of an apple?"

The game warden calmly replied, "Friend, I tried that once, but all I caught was a picture of a rabbit."

The maharaja of an Indian province decreed that no wild animals could be killed. Soon the province was overrun by tigers, lions, panthers, and boars. The people couldn't stand it any longer, so they gave the maharaja the heave-ho. This is the first instance where the reign was called because of the game.

One day a lion came upon a bull wandering in the jungle. He pounced upon the bull, killed him, and ate him. He felt so good afterward that he began to roar. He roared so loud a hunter heard him and came into the jungle and killed the lion.

Moral: When you're full of bull, keep your mouth shut.

A fisherman was lugging a fish twice his size when he met another fisherman with a half dozen very small ones on a string.

"Howdy," said the first fisherman, dropping the huge fish and waiting for a comment.

The second fisherman stared and stared. Then he said, calmly, "Just caught the one, eh?"

"Say, pop, what do I do now?"

FISHERMAN TO BOY: You've been watching me for hours. I bet you do a lot of fishing.
BOY: Nope, none at all.
MAN: Why not?
BOY: I haven't got the time.

D.B.: How was your fishing trip in Texas?
C.D.: Well, I caught one, and he was too small, but luckily two other fishermen came along in a truck and helped me throw him back in.

STRANGER: Catch any fish?
FISHERMAN: Did I! I took forty out of this stream this morning.
STRANGER: Know who I am? I'm the game warden.
FISHERMAN: Know who I am? I'm the biggest liar in the state.

One day three men went bear hunting. They reached a cabin, and each was bragging how good a hunter he was. Early in the morning one of them decided to get the first bear and slipped quietly out of the cabin. He hadn't gone far when he met the biggest, tallest, hungriest-looking bear he'd ever seen. For a moment he just stood there. Then he dropped his gun and ran toward the cabin with the bear close behind him. He opened the cabin door; the bear lunged at him and tripped through the open door. Thinking fast, the hunter shut the door and yelled, "There's the first one, fellows. You skin him, and I'll go get another."

Mrs. Newlywed wanted to prove to her husband that she was a good cook. So she bought a chicken for dinner the next night. She plucked the bird carefully and put it in the roaster with all the trimmings. Three hours later she heard a terrific banging coming from the oven. She opened the roaster, and as she did so, the bird sat up in the roaster and said to the newlywed: "Look, lady, either turn on the oven or give me back my feathers."

TIM: How do you shoot a blue elephant?
JIM: I don't know. How?
TIM: With a blue gun. How do you shoot a white elephant?
JIM: With a white gun?
TIM: No, hold his nose till he turns blue and shoot him with a blue gun.

GUIDE: *That tiger was in just the right spot. Why didn't you shoot it?*
HUNTER: *He didn't have the right expression on his face for a rug.*

GROUSE HUNTER NO. 1: Hey, you hit my wife.
GROUSE HUNTER NO. 2: Sorry, old bean. Have a shot at mine over there.

To study the migratory habits of birds, a government agent released thousands banded with metal strips reading "Notify Fish and Wild Life Division. Wash. Biol. Surv." They soon heard from a Kansas farmer: "Gents, I shot one of your crows last week and followed the instructions attached to it. I washed it, biled it, and surved it. It was awful."

A small boy had fallen into a creek. A young woman got him out and asked him, "How did you come to fall in?"

"I didn't come to fall in. I came to fish," answered the boy.

TOURIST: *Shame on you—a big man like you catching a poor, helpless, little fish.*
FISHERMAN: *Well, if the fish had kept his mouth shut, he wouldn't be on the end of the hook.*

The stranger stopped his car to watch a fisherman on the riverbank. The angler caught a big pike but threw it back. The stranger didn't say a word. Then the fisherman landed a large trout, and threw it back. Finally, he caught a small perch and deposited it in his bag.

"Say," the stranger called out, "why did you keep that small one and throw the two big ones back in?"

The fisherman shrugged. "Small frying pan."

WARDEN: *You can't catch fish without a permit.*
FISHERMAN: *I'm doing fine with just a worm, thank you.*

Zeb and Abe met after a fishing trip. Zeb asked Abe if he had any luck.

"Yup," replied Abe. "I caught me a sixty-five-pound cat. How about you?"

"Nope," answered Zeb, rubbing his whiskers, "but I fished out an old lantern I'd lost ten years ago, and it was still burning."

After a minute or so of silence, Abe looked up at Zeb and said, "Maybe that fish wasn't that big after all. I'll knock off thirty pounds, Zeb, if you'll blow the light out in that lantern."

A new method of catching elephants: Go to elephant country, and find a water hole. With your elephant-catching kit, consisting of a pencil, paper, milk bottle, binoculars, and a pair of tweezers, make a sign that says FOR ELFANTS, *and post it nearby. When the first elephant comes along, he'll see that "elephants" is spelled wrong, and he'll start laughing. The sound of his laughing will bring out the other elephants to see what's happening. When you have a whole herd of elephants, look at them through the wrong end of the binoculars, pick them up with the tweezers, and drop them in the milk bottle.*

A lady who was just married was going to try and please her husband, so she went to the butcher shop and ordered a chicken.

The clerk said, "Do you want a pullet?"

The lady replied, "No, thanks, I'll carry it."

RANDY: *If there were three weasels on a limb and I shot one, how many would be left?*
CHRIS: *Two left.*
RANDY: *Wrong. None would be left. If I shot one, the other two would run away.*
CHRIS: *That's what I said. Two left.*

One day two fathers and sons went fishing. Each fisherman caught a fish. Yet only three fish were caught. How was this possible?

There were only three fishermen—a boy, his father, and his grandfather. The father is counted as a son because his own father was along.

Chapter 4

Hicks and Slickers

"I tell you I won't take this room," protested the old lady to the bellboy. "I'm not going to pay my good money for a measly little room like this. Just because I'm from the country, you can't—"

"Madam," the bellboy said, "this isn't your room. This is the elevator."

The little city boy was on his first real vacation with his father. The two were hiking in the mountains when Daddy pointed out a brilliant rainbow.

"It sure is pretty," said the youngster. "What's it advertising?"

MOUNTAINEER: What'll my boy learn at this here school, teacher?
TEACHER: History, spelling, trigonometry....
MOUNTAINEER: That's fine. Give him lots of that there trigonometry. He's the worst shot in the family.

Then there was the story of the Westerner who entered an eight-year-old horse at an Eastern track. Since the horse had no previous races, he wasn't favored to win. But he galloped home first by several lengths. The stewards, naturally suspicious, called the owner in for questioning.

"How come you never raced this horse before?" they demanded. "After all, you have had him for eight years."

"Well to tell the truth," the Westerner said, sheepishly, "we couldn't catch him until he was seven."

A mountaineer, on his first visit to a town of any size, came to the city with his son. He was fascinated by the asphalt streets.

Scraping his feet on the hard surface, he remarked to the boy, "Well, I can't blame 'em for building a town here. The ground's too hard to plow."

A group of city boys were hiking in the country. One of them came upon a heap of empty milk bottles. In great excitement he yelled to his companions, "Hey, fellas, come here, quick! I found a cow's nest."

"They're bound to break the record. It's set to explode in four minutes."

FIRST FARMER: *Now that Tom has a college degree, can you see any change in the way he plows?*
SECOND FARMER: *No, he plows the same. It's the way he talks.*
FIRST FARMER: *How do you mean that?*
SECOND FARMER: *Well, when he gets to the end of the row, instead of saying, "Whoa, haw, gee," he saps, "Halt, Rebecca, pivot and proceed."*

Chapter 5

Play on Words

TEACHER: What is used as a conductor of electricity?
JOE: Why—er—
TEACHER: Correct, wire. Now, tell me what is the unit of electrical power.
JOE: The what?
TEACHER: Right, the watt.

Did you hear about the glassblower who inhaled? Now he has a pane in his stomach.

JON: I just got home from the dentist.
RON: What did he do?
JON: He was pulling teeth, and he took each nerve out and put them on a rack so he could study them.
RON: Wow! That must be a tedious job.
JON: No—it's nerve-racking.

SERGEANT: *Jones, why didn't you stop when I yelled, "Company, halt."*
ROOKIE JONES: *But, Sarge, I've been here in camp now for two weeks, so I didn't think that you still considered me company.*

Aunt Matilda was wrapping a birthday gift for her nephew.

"What did you give him last year?" asked Uncle George.

"A check," replied Aunt Matilda, "and he said he couldn't find words to thank me."

"What are you giving him now?"

"A dictionary."

JOE: I once went hunting in Africa with only a club.
BILL: You're not that brave.
JOE: I am, too. There were forty in the club.

Sir Lancelot dismounted and rushed into the inn. "My steed is too weary to go on," he said to the landlord. "Can you lend me a horse?"

"I have no horse," replied the landlord, and he pointed to a huge old dog in the corner. "That is the only animal I possess."

"Very well," said Sir Lancelot. "Then I must take him."

"Oh, sir!" cried the landlord. "I wouldn't send a knight out on a dog like this!"

MOTHER: *Betty acts like a furnace when it is time to practice her piano lesson.*
FATHER: *Why? Does she get all steamed up?*
MOTHER: *No, because when I don't watch her, she goes out.*

While making a long, dull speech, a politician received a great deal of heckling from the gallery. Finally, a cabbage landed on the stage and came to rest at his feet.

"Ladies and gentlemen," said the politician, "I see that one of my opponents has lost his head."

RECRUIT (*after physical*): *Well, Doc, how do I stand?*
DOC: *I don't know. It's a mystery to me!*

Nero was talking with one of his officers. "We're not making much money out of this amphitheater," he commented.

"No," sighed the officer. "The lions are eating up all the prophets."

The mother was tucking her four-year-old boy into bed after an especially trying day. "Well," she sighed, "I've certainly worked from son up to son down."

JOE: *Your pants look sad today.*
MIKE: *What do you mean?*
JOE: *Depressed.*

A chip on the shoulder indicates that there is wood higher up.

WIFE: Why did you tear the back pages out of that new book?

ABSENTMINDED DOCTOR: I'm sorry, dear. That section was labeled "Appendix" and I took it out without thinking.

REAL ESTATE AGENT: *Now here is a house without a flaw.*

SOUTH CAROLINA BELLE: *What do y'all walk on?*

BILL: What did the calf say when he looked into the silo?

JOE: I don't know. What?

BILL: Is that my fodder in there?

PAM: Why are you taking your math paper to the gym?

SAM: I have to reduce these fractions.

JIM: *Why couldn't the bowlegged cowboy round up the herd?*

TIM: *I don't know. Why?*

JIM: *He couldn't get his calves together.*

Q: *Why did the golfer wear two pairs of pants to the golf course?*

A: *In case he got a hole in one.*

SAL: *I heard you and Bob ran into each other on your bicycles.*
SUE: *And how! He was knocked speechless, and my front wheel was knocked spokeless.*

JOE: I'm a very funny comedian.
BECKY: What makes you think so?
JOE: I put some of my jokes in the fire and it just roared.

Sir, the enemy soldiers are before us thick as peas. All right, shell them!

HUCK: *Did you tell me you used to make whaling trips with your dad?*
BUCK: *Yes, out to the woodshed.*

A father was teaching his son to play golf. The boy hit his ball into the rough, and it landed on an anthill by chance. The boy started swinging at the ball. He didn't hit the ball, but he killed a lot of ants. Finally, there were only two ants left. One of the ants turned to the other and said, "If we want to live, we've got to get on the ball."

JIM: Why don't you like girls?
JOE: They're too biased.
JIM: Biased? What do you mean?
JOE: It's bias this and bias that till I'm broke.

Mama skunk was worried because she could never keep track of her two children. They were named In and Out. One day she called Out in to her and told him to go out and bring In in. So Out went out and in no time at all he brought In in.

"Wonderful!" said mama skunk. "How in all that great forest could you find him so fast?"

"It was easy," said Out. "In stinct."

DOCTOR: *What is the difference between unlawful and illegal?*
LAWYER: *There isn't any.*
DOCTOR: *Oh, yes there is. Unlawful is against the law, and illegal is a sick bird.*

SHE: If April showers bring May flowers, what do May flowers bring?
HE: What?
SHE: Pilgrims.

Q: If a burglar broke into a cellar, would the coal chute?
A: No, but the kindling wood.

Tongue Twister: As I was passing through Arkansas, I saw a saw that could outsaw any saw I ever saw. Now if you pass through Arkansas and see a saw that can outsaw the saw I saw I'd like to see the saw you saw saw.

An Englishman was persuaded to see his first baseball game. During the play he happened to look away from the field for a moment. Suddenly a foul tip caught him on the ear and knocked him out. On coming to, he asked faintly: "What was it?"

"A foul—only a foul," was the reply.

"Good heavens!" the Englishman exclaimed. "A fowl? I thought it was a mule!"

Two mosquitoes were resting on Robinson Crusoe's back.

"I'm leaving now," said one, "but I'll see you on Friday."

"What is the secret of success?" asked the Sphinx.
"Push," said the button.
"Take pains," said the window.
"Always keep cool," said the ice.
"Be up to date," said the calendar.
"Make light of everything," said the fire.
"Do a driving business," said the hammer.
"Find a good thing and stick to it," said the glue.

Two ants were racing madly across the top of a cracker box. Finally, one of them stopped suddenly and said to his companion, "Hold it. Why are we running so hard?"

The other ant turned around and said, disgustedly, "Look, it says right here. 'Tear across dotted line.'"

TOM: *What is the Eskimo song?*
JANE: *Fr——eeze a jolly good fellow.*

TEACHER: What are the people of New York noted for?
STUDENT: Their stupidity.
TEACHER: Where did you get that idea?
STUDENT: It says in my book that the population of New York is very dense.

FRED: *Why do you say amen in a church instead of awomen?*
TED: *I don't know, why?*
FRED: *Because you sing hymns, not hers.*

JOE: In one word, can you define a bull that swallowed a bomb?
MOE: No. How do you?
JOE: Abominable.
JOE: How about if it exploded?
MOE: No. What would it be?
JOE: Noble.

A couple visiting Russia hired a man named Rudolph as a guide. One day as they were walking along, the husband remarked that it was snowing, but Rudolph said it was raining. The husband asked his wife whether she thought it was snow or rain, and she replied: "It must be rain because Rudolph, the Red, knows rain, dear."

Two buckets met each other in the street. One bucket said: "You're a little pail."

"Yes," the other replied, "I'm not a well bucket."

TEACHER: Dick, what is the formula for water?
DICK: H I J K L M N O.
TEACHER: Are you trying to be funny?
DICK: No, you told us that the formula for water was H to O.

Q: What is an expert?
A: "X" is a mathematical term used to denote something unknown. "Spurt" is a drip of water under pressure. Therefore, an Xspurt is an unknown drip under pressure.

TED: How's business?
TAILOR: Just sew-sew.
ELECTRICIAN: It's pretty light.
FARMER: Mine is growing.
ASTRONOMER: It's looking up.
OPTICIAN: It's looking better.
AUTHOR: Mine is all write.

What is the difference between Prince Charles, an orphan, a bald-headed man, and a gorilla?

Prince Charles is an heir apparent; an orphan has ne'er a parent; a bald-headed man has no hair apparent; and a gorilla has a hairy parent.

Q: What flower describes what the professor did when he sat on a tack?
A: Rose.

BILL: *My dog swallowed a flashlight last night.*
JOHN: *Is he sick?*
BILL: *No, he spit it out, and now he's delighted.*

Q: What did the food say when it was leftover and rewrapped for the third time.
A: Curses, foiled again.

MOTHER: Ronnie, did you make your bed?
RONNIE: Yes, Mother, but I still think that we should have bought one instead.

Flattery is soft soap, and soft soap is 90 percent lye.

TOM: What did the colt say when it was asked to make a speech?
JACK: I don't know.
TOM: You'll have to excuse me—I'm just a little hoarse.

Q: Why did the germ cross the microscope?
A: To get to the other slide.

JOE: What animal is a cannibal?
MOE: I don't know.
JOE: A cow. It eats its fodder.

CLASS PRESIDENT: Congratulate me. I won the election.
POP: Honestly?
CLASS PRESIDENT: Oh, why bring that up?

TED: *Why are you doing your painting all bundled up like that?*
JED: *Well, it says right here on the paint can to be sure to put on three coats.*

MIKE: What did one magnet say to the other magnet?
JOE: I don't know.
MIKE: You're very attractive today.

Q: If a cat ate a lemon, what would it be?
A: A sourpuss.

MIT: Why is the nose in the middle of the face?
WIT: Because it's the scenter.

JIM: *What is the difference between a cat and a comma?*
JOHN: *I don't know.*
JIM: *A cat has claws at the end of its paws, and a comma has a pause at the end of its clause.*

SENIOR (*at basketball game*): See that big substitute down there playing forward? I think he's going to be our best man next year.
COED: Oh, dear, this is so sudden.

Seven days of dieting make one weak.

A Peace Corps representative was sent to a cannibal tribe. When the chief was asked what was learned, he said, "We had a slight taste of democracy."

Q: Why did the fly fly?
A: Because the spider spied'er.

A tree surgeon's son wanted to go into business in a small way, so he opened a branch office.

A candlestick maker has it easy—he only works on wick ends.

RANDY: *What would happen if you swallowed uranium?*
ANDY: *You'd get atomic ache.*

Chapter 6

Daffynitions

Dancing: The art of pulling your feet away faster than your partner can step on them.

No-hitter: A pitcher who can throw a ball faster than you can shake a stick at it.

Golf ball: A small, round, object which remains on the tee while a perspiring citizen fans it vigorously with a large club.

Horsefly: A fly with laryngitis.

Vacation: That time when a man stops doing what his boss wants him to do and does what his wife wants him to do.

Ginger ale: A drink that tastes the way your foot feels when it goes to sleep.

Beatles: Barbershop quartet that did not get waited on.

Drizzle: A drip going steady.

Minuteman: A fellow who can make it to the refrigerator and back while the commercial is on.

Snowbank: Where Eskimos keep their money.

Binoculars: Parasites.

Intense: Where Boy Scouts sleep.

Skiing: Something a person learns in several sittings.

Muggy day: A time when everything that's supposed to stick together comes apart, and everything that's supposed to come apart sticks together.

Describe: De guy takes de minutes of de meeting.

Horse sense: Stable thinking.

Bathing beauty: A girl worth wading for.

Pasteurize: Up to your forehead.

Caterpillar: A worm wearing a sweater.

Pole vault: Safe where lumber is kept.

Intellectual: Someone who can listen to the "William Tell Overture" without thinking of the Lone Ranger.

Poker: Something you do to a mule to get her to go.

Melancholy: Watermelon watchdog.

Exit: What a teacher does to a wrong answer.

Wooden nickel: Oaken token.

Heroes: What a Boy Scout does to a boat.

Generally: Head of the Confederate army.

Information: How Air Force planes fly.

Mischief: The chief's daughter.

Chapter 7

Just for Laughs

Once upon a time a mother sheep wanted her lambs to go to school. The first day when they came home she asked them what they had learned. The first one said "Baa-a-a," and the mother sheep was tickled. Then she asked the other one what he learned, and he said, "Moo-o-o, I'm taking a foreign language."

Did you hear about the guy who crossed a crocodile with an abalone? He was trying to get an abadile, but all that he could get was a crocobalone.

Sign on the door of a basketball coach's office: "The frame of this door is six feet three inches high. If you can enter without ducking your head—DON'T."

MOTHER TIGER: *Junior, what are you doing?*
JUNIOR: *I'm chasing a hunter around the tree.*
MOTHER TIGER: *Stop that! How many times have I told you not to play with your food?*

"I'm sorry," said the dentist to the patient, "but I can't give you an appointment this afternoon. I have eighteen cavities to fill." Whereupon he picked up his golf bag and left for the course.

Famous saying among those in the chicken restaurant business, "If at first you don't fricassee, fry, fry a hen."

Sign on a newly painted school wall: "This is a partition, not a petition. No signatures required."

A high school boy took home from the library a book whose cover read How to Hug, *only to discover it was Volume 7 of the encyclopedia.*

A gentleman was barbecuing a chicken on a spit in his backyard. He kept turning the spit handle around and around. Watching from the sidewalk was a beatnik, who finally said, "I don't want to bug you, dad, but your music's stopped, and your monkey's on fire."

IKE: *Is that a real diamond ring?*
MIKE: *If it isn't, I've been cheated out of twenty-nine cents.*

A gorilla walked into a drugstore and ordered a 50-cent sundae. He put down a $10 bill to pay for it. The clerk thought, *Gorillas don't know much about money*, and handed the animal a $1 bill in change. The clerk's curiosity got the best of him, and he said, "We don't get too many gorillas in here." The gorilla replied, "No wonder, at nine dollars a sundae."

PRIVATE: Sir, an urgent message just came from our desert outpost requesting water.
CAPTAIN: A caravan is scheduled to arrive there two days from now. They can surely hold out that long.
PRIVATE: I don't think so, sir. The stamp was stuck on the envelope with a paper clip.

A man walked into a diner in a strange town and was asked by the waitress what he wanted.

"Two fried eggs and a kind word," he answered.

The waitress said nothing but went inside to give the order. When she came back with his order, the out-of-towner said, "Thanks for the eggs, but how about the kind word?"

The waitress leaned over and whispered: "Don't eat those eggs."

Mr. Smith took his nephew to the ballet. The little boy watched the ballerinas dancing on tiptoe awhile, then turned to his uncle and asked, "Why don't they just get taller girls?"

JOE: *How do you spell weather?*
MOE: *Wqrstv.*
JOE: *That's the worst spell of weather we've had in a long time.*

Upon finishing their dinner in a restaurant, a young mother beckoned to the waiter and asked him to wrap up the leftover steak for their dog at home. Whereupon her little boy spoke up, "Oh, boy! We're finally going to get a dog!"

A few drops of rain fell just before a Texas drought was broken. Several of them hit a friend of mine in the face, and he fainted from shock. I had to throw several buckets of sand on him to bring him to.

Once a superintendent of schools was visiting a small three-room school. One room was very noisy, but he just sat there patiently.

Finally, the man got up, opened the door, and grabbed a tall boy who had been standing up talking. He then took the boy into the other room and stood him in the corner. Five minutes later a small boy came out of the first room and said: "When can we have our teacher back?"

A letter from a college boy to his father:
"Dear Dad: No mon, no fun. Your Son."
The reply: "Too bad, so sad. Your Dad."

Small boy, explaining broken window to policeman: "I was cleaning my slingshot, and it went off."

One morning a farmer called his new hired man at 4 A.M. for breakfast. After breakfast he said, "It's a little early, so let's eat lunch so we won't have to stop this noon." So they ate their lunch.

After they finished the lunch, the farmer said, "We might as well eat our supper so we can work until dark."

After they ate that meal, the hired man started to take off his shoes. The farmer said, "What's the big idea?"

The hired man replied, "I usually go to bed right after supper."

A Chicago family was having dinner when the phone rang. The maid answered and said, "It sure is!" and hung up. The same thing happened five minutes later.

"What's going on?" asked the father.

"Some crackpot," explained the maid, "keeps calling to say, 'It's long distance from New York.'"

FARM BOY: My father doesn't know whether to get a cow or a tractor.

CITY BOY: He'd sure look funny trying to ride a cow.

FARM BOY: He'd look even funnier trying to milk a tractor.

Two not-so-talkative Maine farmers had known each other all their lives, but their conversations were limited. One afternoon, however, one grew loquacious: "Hey, Luke, what did you give your horse when he had that colic?" "Turpentine," replied Luke. Two weeks later they met again. "Didn't you tell me, Luke, that you gave your sick horse turpentine?" "Yup," said Luke. "Well, I gave mine some and he died." "So did mine," answered Luke.

"Doctor," said the patient, "I can't say why, but I get sort of a pain I don't know where, and it leaves me in a kind of a—sort of a—well, I don't know what."

The doctor replied thoughtfully. "Here's a prescription for I don't know what. Take it for I don't know how many times a day for I don't know how long, and you'll feel better I don't know when."

An old Indian wrapped in a blanket sat watching a typical television Western with a wagon train besieged by thousands of painted warriors. Just as the U.S. cavalry conveniently arrived with colors flying and bugles blaring, the Indian leaped up and ran out the door.

When he returned a few minutes later, someone asked, "What scared you, Indian? The U.S. cavalry to the rescue?"

"No," answered the Indian. "A policeman standing near my car."

Then there was an old farmer who bragged that his land was more fertile than anyone else's. He claimed that his watermelons were so big that he could not get them into his wagon. Then one day a man from a Boy Scout camp wanted to buy 100 pounds of potatoes. But this farmer said that he would not cut one of his potatoes in half for anyone.

Two men from Mars, the first to land on Earth, were very excited as they stepped out of their spaceship near a large town. Pointing to the TV aerials on almost every house, one happily said to the other: "Look, girls."

The sports car racer was giving a friend his first ride in one of the low-slung models. The friend appeared to be puzzled, so the driver asked what was wrong.

"I can't figure out what that long wall is that we've been passing."

"That's no wall," snapped the driver. "It's the curb."

The lightning bug is brilliant,
But it hasn't any mind.
It blunders through existence,
With its headlight on behind.

Football player: "I shot a pass into the air, it fell to earth I know not where, and that is why I sit and dream, on the bench with the second team."

I wish I were a kangaroo
Despite his funny stances.
I'd have a place to put the junk
My girl brings to the dances.

Answering the doorbell, a housewife tripped over a cap pistol and picked it up. She had it when she opened the door for a salesman. He looked at her, turned pale, and ran, jumping a three-foot fence. The housewife then discovered a sign on her door, put there by her son because she had said she was annoyed with salesmen. It read: "We shoot every third salesman, and the second one just left."

Two members of the beat generation went to the seashore to watch the flight of an experimental Navy jet. During the flight a button was pressed on a new automatic ejection seat, and the co-pilot floated down to earth in his parachute. "Man," said one of the beats, "dig that crazy toaster."

The jockey explained that he won his races by singing to the horses while they were running. He had phenomenal success, and after a while someone asked exactly what he sang that made them run so fast.

"Well," he said. "I use a different tune all the time, but the words are always the same.

"Roses are red, violets are blue, horses that lose are made into glue."

FARMER: You must be brave to come down in a hundred-mile gale like this in a parachute.
SOLDIER: I didn't come down like this in a chute. I went up in a tent.

Once two goats were in a movie projection booth. One of the goats saw a can of film and ate it.
The other goat said: "How did you like the film?"
The first goat replied, "It was okay, but I liked the book better!"

An old Indian stood on a hilltop with his son, looking over a beautiful valley below. After a period of silence the old Indian spoke, "Someday, my son, all this land will belong to the Indians again. White man all go to moon."

RALPH: Did you know that a grasshopper can jump four times its length?
SAM: No, but I have seen a wasp lift a two-hundred-pound man four feet off the ground.

Distraught mother to a group of wild children at a birthday party: "There is a special prize for the one who goes home first."

SALLY: I'm disgusted!
JAN: Why?
SALLY: I stepped on a weighing machine and it said, "One person at a time."

"Well, you made better time than I thought you would."

A weary traveler came to an inn and said, "I want a room."

The innkeeper replied: "There's only one room left, and that's where the white-eyed ghost lives."

The traveler answered, "I'll take it because I don't believe in ghosts."

After going to his room, he heard a scary "Boooooo, I'm the white-eyed ghost." The traveler said, "You'd better be quiet or you'll be the black-eyed ghost!"

Two Alaskans were fighting when this Texan tried to get a word in. One Alaskan snapped, "Shut up, or we'll cut Alaska in two and make Texas the third largest state."

"Please, lady, for a nickel I'll have my brother imitate a hen for you."

"And how does he do that, my little man?" the lady asked. "Cackle?"

"No, ma'am," the boy said. "None of those cheap imitations. I'll have him eat a worm."

There was a young woman named Flynn who grew so exceedingly thin that when she tried to drink lemonade, she slipped through the straw and fell in.

The doctor went up to visit the sick woman but came down in a few minutes to ask her husband for a screwdriver. A few minutes later he was down again and asked for a can opener. Still later he was back for a chisel and a hammer. The worried husband couldn't stand it any longer.

"Please tell me what's wrong with my wife, Doc," he cried.

"Don't know yet," replied the doctor. "I can't get the lock of my bag open."

TEX: We really had a dry year in Texas.
JOE: You did?
TEX: It got so hot and dry and my cows got so skinny that I could brand two cows at once.
JOE: How could you do that?
TEX: By putting a piece of carbon paper in between 'em.

One day a man came walking down the street with his dog, which had a real long snoot. Another man came out of his house and said, "You had better get your dog out of here because my bulldog will come out and eat your dog all up." The bulldog came out and the little dog ate the bulldog all up.

The one man said, "What kind of dog is that?"

The other man said, "Well, before I cut off his tail and painted him yellow, he was an alligator."

At a small garden party the young wife whispered to her husband, "That's the fourth time you've gone back for more ice cream and cake. Doesn't it embarrass you?"

"Why should it?" asked the husband. "I keep telling them it's for you."

A man was invited to a friend's bridge party. When he arrived, he noticed a dog sitting at the table playing bridge with them.

After observing the dog for a while, he remarked: "That's a pretty smart dog you have there."

His friend replied, "Naw, he's really very stupid. Every time he gets a good hand he wags his tail."

In the parlor there were three—
He, the candlelight, and she—
Three's a crowd, there is no doubt,
So the candlelight went out.

After the barber had cut, nicked, and gashed him, he asked for a glass of water.

The barber said "What's the matter—do you feel faint?"

"No," he said, "I just want to see if my mouth still holds water."

Two young boys were leaving the cafeteria, and as they passed the cashier's desk, one paid his bill, but the second one handed the cashier a slip of paper with the number 1004180 on it. The cashier studied the number a moment, then let the young man pass without paying.

Can you figure out why he didn't have to pay?
A. 1004180 means "I owe nothing, for I ate nothing."

It was April, and the father of the household called the telephone company and ordered a 50-foot extension cord put on the phone. He explained: "Now that spring is here and the weather is nice, I want my daughter to stay outdoors more."

"When does the library open?" the voice on the phone asked.

"At nine A.M.," came the reply. "And what's the idea of calling me in the middle of the night?"

"Not until nine A.M.?" said the disappointed voice.

"No, not until nine," answered the librarian. "Why do you want to get in before nine A.M.?"

"Who wants to get in? I want to get out."

HUSBAND: *Dear, I have tickets for the theater.*
WIFE: *Splendid. I'll start dressing at once.*
HUSBAND: *Yes, do. The tickets are for tomorrow night.*

HARRY: I got the prize for being best student in natural history.
LARRY: How come?
HARRY: The teacher asked how many legs an ostrich had, and I said three.
LARRY: But an ostrich has only two legs.
HARRY: Well, all the rest of the class said four.

SLIM: How do you like art class, Jim?
JIM: Fine, but I wish we had a smarter art teacher. Today I drew a horse, and she didn't know what it was.

Two men were taking an ocean cruise. One man suddenly said to the other, "Hey, man, look at all that water."

The second man replied, "Yeah, and that's only the top."

An old Indian took his watch to a jeweler for the first time to have it repaired. The jeweler took the watch apart, and a dead insect fell out. The Indian, noticing the dead bug lying on the table, said, "Ugh! No wonder watch no run, engineer dead."

The bus was already crowded when the fat woman entered. She stood for a moment glaring at the seated passengers. "Isn't some gentleman going to offer me his seat?" she asked.

At this, one exceptionally small man rose. "Well," he said, rather shyly, "I'm willing to make a small contribution."

"So your father can lick my father. What's so great about that? My mother can lick him, too!"

Mountain climbers rope themselves together because there is safety in numbers—also to keep the sensible ones from going home.

A recruit was on guard duty with specific orders to admit no car to the area unless it bore a special tag. The sentry stopped a tagless car carrying a high-ranking officer. Hearing the officer order his driver to go right on through, the guard asked calmly, "I'm new at this, sir. Do I shoot you or the driver?"

An Indian once asked a judge to give him a shorter name. "What is your name now?" asked the judge.

"Chief Big Screeching Train Whistle," answered the Indian.

"And what do you want to shorten it to?" asked the judge.

The Indian folded his arms and said, "Toots."

A farmer and his wife went to a fair. The farmer was interested in the airplanes, and finally asked a pilot how much a ride cost. The pilot said $10 for ten minutes. The farmer said that was very expensive, so the pilot remarked, "I'll make you a deal. If you and your wife can go for a ride for ten minutes and not make a sound, it won't cost you a thing. However, if you make one sound, you have to pay the ten dollars."

They went for the ride, and after the pilot landed, he said, "I want to congratulate you for not making even one sound. You are a very brave man."

The farmer then said, "Well, maybe so, but I almost yelled when my wife fell out."

Then there was the one about the absentminded professor who fell down the flight of stairs. He picked himself up, brushed himself off, looked up the stairs questioningly, and remarked, "I wonder what all that racket was about?"

When Abe Lincoln was canvassing some of his Illinois neighbors for their votes, he encountered a crusty old farmer who was bitterly opposed to him.

"Vote for you?" shouted the old man. "Why, I'd sooner vote for the devil."

"I'm sure you would," replied Lincoln calmly, "but in case your friend doesn't run, maybe you would give your vote to me."

Russian Theme Song: You'll wonder where your father went if he talks about the government.

One day the veteran sergeant gathered his new recruits into the barracks to give them a lecture. He finished his impromptu orientation saying, "No matter how dirty or distasteful the job you're ordered to do is, or how much of a bawling out you get, just remember that you always have the right to the last word."

The sergeant paused for a second to let this unbelievable little morsel of information sink in. Then he added: "That last word is 'Yessir.'"

Three weary men went to their hotel from work one day to find the elevator out of order. All three men lived on the seventy-third floor of the building. To pass the time, the first man would sing, the second would tell a joke, and the third would tell a sad story. So the first man sang, the second told a joke, and upon reaching the seventy-second floor, all the third man said was, "I forgot the key."

A fat man and a skinny man were arguing about who was the more courteous. The skinny man said he was more courteous because he always tipped his hat to ladies. But the fat man knew he was the more courteous because whenever he got up and offered his seat, two ladies could sit down.

In the dim light of a Hollywood café I studied the menu without finding anything that appealed to me. Glancing across the aisle, I saw a woman contemplating an inviting looking salad on the table before her, refreshingly green and delightfully garnished.
"Bring me the same salad that woman over there has, please," I said to the waiter.
The waiter looked and then bent over and whispered confidentially, "Sir, that is the lady's hat."

PATIENT: Doctor, if there is anything wrong with me, don't frighten me by giving it a long scientific name. Just tell me in plain words.
DOCTOR: Well, to be frank about it, it's just plain laziness.
PATIENT: Thanks, now give me the scientific name, so I can tell them at home.

MA: Pa, I don't think the neighbors like the new drum we got Johnny for Christmas.
PA: Why not?
MA: They gave him a knife and asked him if he knew what was in the drum.

On a flight over the Rocky Mountains, an airline hostess distributed chewing gum to the passengers.

"It's to keep your ears from popping at high altitude," she explained.

When the plane landed, one of the passengers rushed up to the hostess and said, "I'm meeting my wife right away. How do I get the gum out of my ears?"

There was once a fellow who would snap his fingers whenever he talked. His wife finally got tired of this and sent him to a psychiatrist. The psychiatrist asked the man whether he was happy. The man answered yes and snapped his fingers. Finally, the psychiatrist asked, "Why do you snap your fingers?"

"To keep the elephants away," was the reply.

"But there aren't any elephants within two thousand miles of here," said the psychiatrist.

"See, it works," replied the man.

In the days of the Old West a two gun badman roared into a saloon one day, shooting in all directions.

Standing in the middle of the floor he shouted, "All you dirty bums get out of here."

In two minutes the place was empty except for one old man calmly smoking his pipe.

The badman swaggered over to the old man. "Well?" he said.

The old man looked at the bandit calmly. "Sure was a lot of 'em, wasn't there?"

I love to do my homework,
It makes me feel so good;
I love to do exactly
As my teachers say I should;
I love my schoolwork very much,
I never miss a day;
And I even love the men in white
Who are taking me away.

A fighter staggered back to his corner after taking a terrific beating in the seventh round. His manager whispered in his ear, "Don't give up now, Sluggo, you've got a no-hitter going!"

Three cellmates in a Russian prison were talking about why they were there. The first one said, "I was accused of absenteeism for being late to work."

The second said, "I came to work early and was accused of being a spy.

The third man looked up from his cot and said: "I came to work on time, and they accused me of buying an American watch."

A ship banged into the stern of another vessel but did no real harm. After maneuvering away, it rammed the same ship again. Thinking that now he had done real damage to the other ship, the captain signaled: "Can you stay afloat?"

"Yes," flashed the other skipper. "Would you like to try again?"

A man came out to install the hillbilly's new TV set. "Now this," he said, pointing to the antenna, "will have to go on the roof."

"It's like I always said, Zeke," said the lady of the house to her husband. "One thing leads to another. Now we have to put a roof on the house."

Three turtles decided to have a cup of coffee. Just as they got into the café, it started to rain. The biggest turtle said to the smallest turtle: "Go home and get the umbrella."

The little one replied, "I will, if you don't drink my coffee."

"We won't," the other two promised.

Two years later the big turtle said to the middle turtle, "Well, I guess he isn't coming back, so we might as well drink his coffee."

Just then a voice called from outside the door, "If you do, I won't go."

Not a man on the bus rose to give the package-laden woman a seat. One middle-aged man, however, was more thoughtful than the others. He tugged at her sleeve and whispered: "Be on your toes at Pine Boulevard, lady. That's where I get off."

A teen-ager sent his girlfriend her first orchid with this note: "With all my love and most of my allowance."

He asked me: When? I could not tell.
He queried: Who? Again I fell.
He named a man, to me a stranger,
And I could see myself in danger.
What was this plight—this mystery?
Oh, just my course in history.

An Englishman of nobility, just arrived in this country, noticed that his clothes had been attacked by moths. He stopped in at a drugstore, and asked the clerk what he could recommend against moths. He was given a box of mothballs, which he took to his hotel.

In a little while he returned for another box and still later another. This time the clerk could not contain his curiosity and asked, "May I ask what you are doing with all those mothballs?"

"Well, my good man," answered His Lordship, "you can't hit the little beggars every time."

Two hermits lived in a cave far from civilization. One day a little dog ran past the entrance to the cave. Six months later one hermit said to the other one, "That was a cute little black dog."

One year later the other hermit said, "It wasn't a black dog; it was a white one."

Eight months later the first hermit jumped up and exclaimed, "If we're going to have this constant bickering, I'm leaving."

"I have a pain in my abdomen," said the rookie to the Army doctor.

"Young man," replied the medico, "officers have abdomens, sergeants have stomachs, you have a bellyache."

A man telephoned a pest exterminator and said he was having trouble with termites. "I can't afford to hire you to get rid of the termites," the man said, "but I'll be grateful if you will give me some free advice."

"I'll gladly give you some free advice," the exterminator replied. "Don't take any wooden nickels."

While waiting to be served in a fashionable restaurant a customer tied his napkin around his neck in bib fashion. This distressed the manager so much that he told a waiter to indicate to the customer, as tactfully as possible, that this simply was not done in the restaurant.

The waiter walked to the table, and in as polite a tone as he could manage, he asked, "What'll it be, sir, shave or a haircut?"

President of the firm to executives: "All opposed will signify by saying, 'I resign.'"

MOTHER: *How did you get this way playing baseball?*
BOY: *Oh, I didn't get this way playing baseball. I was third base.*

WOMAN: *Can you honestly say you didn't take that apple from your little sister?*
BOY: *That's right.*
WOMAN: *But I saw you do it.*
BOY: *Maybe. But she isn't my sister.*

A Navy recruit had neglected to bring in his rifle from the firing range. When he went back for it, he couldn't find it. When he was told he'd have to pay for the rifle, he protested, "Suppose I was driving a Navy jeep and somebody stole it. Would I have to pay for that, too?" He was informed that he would have to pay for all government property he lost.

"Now," the recruit said, "I know why the captain always goes down with his ship."

The cast and crew were on location in Arizona making a movie. One day an old Indian walked up to the director and said, "Tomorrow rain."

And the next day it rained.

The director immediately hired the Indian at $150 a week to predict the weather. However, after a few successful predictions, the Indian didn't show up for several days.

Finally, the director sent a man for the Indian, and they returned in a short while.

"What's the weather going to be like tomorrow?" the director asked.

"Don't know," said the Indian. "Radio broke down. Not work."

JIM: What is the difference between a barber and a mother with several children?

JOHN: A barber has a razor to shave, and a mother has shavers to raise.

OLD LADY: Little girl, your brother has been crying for ten minutes. Can't you cheer him up?

GIRL: Did you ever try to cheer up someone who's just eaten five bananas, three hot dogs, and seven ice-cream cones?

Busy Executive: Miss Smith, where's my pencil?

Secretary: It's behind your ear.

Executive: Come, come. You know I'm a busy man. Which ear?

As the Lone Ranger and Tonto were riding along one day toward the north, a war party of about fifty Indians came at them, so they turned to the south. But another war party came at them. Afraid now, they turned east, but met another party of five hundred Indians. They turned west as a last resort, but there were still more Indians. Then the Lone Ranger turned and said, "Well, Tonto, this is the end. I guess we're goners."

Then Tonto said, "What do you mean, we, paleface?"

TOM: Hey, Tim, have you heard about the baby that drank elephant's milk for one week and gained ten pounds?
TIM: No! Whose baby was it?
TOM: The elephant's.

The sultan got sore at his harem,
And invented a scheme for to scare 'em.
He caught him a mouse,
Which he loosed in the house,
The confusion is called Harem-Scarem.

Mrs. McTavish looked out the window as the family was going in to dinner and wailed, "Och, Jon, here comes company, and I bet they haven't eaten yet."

"Quick," ordered the Scotsman. "Everybody out on the porch with toothpicks."

The absentminded professor was awakened from a deep sleep by the ringing of his telephone at two o'clock in the morning. Stumbling out of bed, he picked up the receiver only to hear a voice at the other end ask, "Is this one, one, one, one?"

"No," mumbled the professor, "This is number eleven eleven."

"Oh, please pardon me," said the voice, "I'm sorry that I disturbed you."

"Not at all," replied the professor. "I had to get up to answer the phone anyway."

A sailor's wife approached the pastor of her church just as he was stepping into the pulpit and handed him a note which read, "Albert Morse, having gone to sea, his wife requests the congregation to pray for his safety."

The minister hastily unfolded the note, and with his mind on the sermon he was about to make, he announced, "Albert Morse, having gone to see his wife, requests the congregation to pray for his safety."

The bull had caught the hired man halfway across the pasture and chased him into a tree. After being rescued, the hired man was saying: "Just as I felt his horns on the seat of my pants, I leaped for a low-hanging branch—about twenty feet off the ground."

"Did you make it?" someone asked.

"Not on the way up," the hired man replied, "but fortunately I grabbed it coming down."

JIM: *How would you get the measurement four gallons if you only had a five-gallon and a three-gallon bucket?*

TIM: *I don't know.*

JIM: *Fill the five-gallon bucket, and from it pour three gallons into the three-gallon bucket. Then there are two gallons left; pour out the water in the three-gallon bucket and pour the remaining two gallons into the three-gallon bucket. Then fill the five-gallon bucket and pour one gallon into the three-gallon bucket.*

Mother sending small boy off to birthday party: "And don't forget: when the party is over, go up to Lucy's mama and apologize."

Joe was having trouble getting up in the morning, so his doctor prescribed some pills. Joe took them, slept well, and was awake before he heard the alarm. He took his time getting to the office, strolled in, and said to his boss: "I didn't have a bit of trouble getting up this morning."

"That's fine," said the boss, "but where were you yesterday?"

When the pioneers settled the country, the Indians were running it. There were no taxes. There was no national debt. The women did all the work—and the pioneers thought they could improve a system like that.

When the four fifteen local from Squeedunk suddenly stopped in the middle of its run, the conductor reassured the passengers: "Just a cow on the tracks."

A few miles farther on, the train squealed to a halt again. Explained the harassed conductor: "We caught up to that cow again."

The young couple had been a little hard pressed for money, and the bride had been preparing chopped meat in as many different ways as she knew.

During the second week she served still another version. As the husband surveyed it wearily, he murmured, "How now, ground cow?"

A newly rich woman was trying to make an impression. "I clean my diamonds with ammonia, my rubies with wine, my emeralds with brandy, and my sapphires with fresh milk."

"I don't clean mine," said the quiet woman next to her. "When mine get dirty, I just throw them away."

A newly married couple were leaving the church in a horse-drawn carriage. The horse stumbled on a rock. "That's one," said the groom. Later on the horse stumbled again. "That's two," he said. A while later the horse tripped on a rock. "That's three," the man said as he pulled out a gun and shot the horse. His wife said he was too cruel. "That's one," said the man, and they lived happily ever after.

A man riding horseback saw a little dog trotting along the road.

"Good morning," said the dog.

"Good morning," the man replied.

As the dog went on down the road, the man remarked aloud, "I didn't know dogs could talk."

"I didn't either," agreed the horse.

The dictator was breathing his last. By his bedside stood his second-in-command, tears streaming down his face. The old dictator patted his aide's hand feebly.

"Don't grieve so, comrade," he whispered. "For your loyalty I leave you my money, my cars, my plane, my yacht—everything."

"Thank you, thank you!" cried the man. "You're so good to me. Oh, if there were only something I could do for you!"

The dying man boosted himself up a bit. "There is," he gasped. "Take your foot off the oxygen tube."

One caveman to another: "Say what you will, we never had this crazy weather until they started using those bows and arrows."

A proud sixteen-year-old boy turned into a driveway at the wheel of the family car. Several younger brothers came up to the car.

"I passed my driver's test," shouted the teen-ager. "You guys can all move up one bike."

One day an old white-haired man was walking down the street and saw a little boy trying to ring a doorbell.

The old man walked up to the boy and rang the bell for him. Then he asked the boy, "What next?"

"Well," the little fellow said, "I don't know about you, but I'm going to start running."

A wife apologized to her husband for buying an expensive fur coat. "Well, why did you do it?" asked the husband.

"Satan tempted me."

"Why didn't you say, 'Get thee behind me, Satan'?"

"I did, but he looked over my shoulder and said, 'Fits you real good in the back, too.'"

In 1952, while returning from Europe by boat, a man dropped a very valuable diamond ring overboard. Last week, while attending a banquet at which fish was served, he bit down on something hard. It was a fishbone.

BOY (*walking into feedstore*): *Mithter, do you thell bird theed?*
SALESMAN: *Son, come back when you can talk better.*
Two weeks later.
BOY: *Mithter, do you thell bird theed?*
SALESMAN: *Look, son, I told you to come back when you learned to speak better. Come back later.*
Three weeks later.
BOY: *Mithter, do you want to buy a dead bird?*

An African chieftain flew to London for a visit and was met at the airport by newsmen.

"Good morning, Chief," one of the newsmen said. "Did you have a comfortable flight?"

The chieftain made a series of raucous noises—honk, oink, screech, whistle, z-z—then added in perfect English, "Yes, very pleasant indeed."

"And how long do you plan to stay?" asked the reporter.

Prefacing his remarks with same odd noises, the chief answered the question, again in perfect English.

"Tell me, Chief," inquired the baffled reporter, "where did you learn to speak such perfect English?"

After the now-standard honks and screeches, the chieftain said, "Shortwave radio."

"No, madam," said the official at City Hall, "I don't know where you can buy a thousand roaches and ten thousand ants. Why do you want them?"

"I'm moving tomorrow," replied the lady, "and my landlord says that I must leave the place exactly as I found it."

A teacher had just handed some exam papers back to her class. "Now," she asked, "does anyone have any questions?"

"Yes," one boy spoke up. "I can't read what you've written at the bottom of my paper."

"It says," answered the teacher, squinting at the paper, "you must learn to write more clearly."

"Listen, Captain," said the perspiring police officer, *"we've been giving that ventriloquist the third degree for over an hour. So far a plainclothesman, three patrolmen, and a sergeant have confessed to the crime. Shall we go on?"*

Introducing the late Thomas A. Edison at a dinner, the toastmaster mentioned his many inventions, dwelling at length on the talking machine. The old inventor said gently: "I thank the gentleman for his kind remarks, but I must insist upon a correction. God invented the talking machine. I only invented the first one that can be shut off."

A little boy was practicing his violin while his father, tired from a hard day's work, was reading the evening newspaper. The family dog, lying on the floor in front of the father, began to howl dismally in rhythm with the scratching violin.

The father endured the combination of dog and violin as long as he could, but soon it was too much for the human ear to stand. Jumping up, he slammed his newspaper to the floor and yelled: "For heaven's sake, can't you play something the dog doesn't know?"

TEACHER: Give me a sentence with an object.
STUDENT: You're very beautiful, teacher.
TEACHER: What's the object?
STUDENT: A good grade.

A lean young man, and rather handsome, too, showed up at a movie studio for a job in western movies. He had a letter that showed he was an expert rider.

"Tenor or baritone?" asked the casting director.

"I can't sing," said the applicant, "but I can ride anything on four legs."

"Play a guitar or banjo?" continued the studio executive.

"No. But I'm not stage-shy. I've made most of the big rodeos, and I rode in Madison Square Garden four times."

"Perhaps you play the accordion?"

"Nope," responded the young man, "I can't play anything. But, mister, give me a rope and I'll show—"

The casting director waved him out impatiently, and he grumbled at him, "And you call yourself a cowboy. . . ."

A High School Student's Seven Rules for Being Popular:
1. *Own a car.*
2. *Be a good conversationalist.*
3. *Own a car.*
4. *Own a car.*
5. *Present a good personal appearance.*
6. *Own a car.*
7. *If the car is a red convertible, rules 2 and 5 can be disregarded.*

Q: How do you carve an elephant out of a piece of stone?
A: Chip away everything that doesn't look like an elephant.

"*If I cut a beefsteak in two,*" asked the teacher of a boy in her arithmetic class, "*then cut the halves in two, what do I get?*"

"Quarters," answered the boy.

"Good," said the teacher. "And then if I cut it again?"

"Eighths."

"Correct. Cut it again?"

"Sixteenths."

"Exactly. And cut it again?"

"Thirty-seconds."

"And once more?"

"Hamburger!" cried the boy impatiently.

WAITRESS: We have practically everything on the menu.

CUSTOMER: So I see. Now, would you bring me a clean one?

TEACHER: *Mathematics is a very exact science. For example, if one man can build a garage in twelve days, twelve men can build it in one day.*

JOHNNY: *Then if one ship can cross the ocean in eight days, I suppose eight ships can cross in one day.*

GROCER: Take a handful of candy.
LITTLE BOY (*shopping with his mother*): No, thank you.
GROCER: Whoever heard of a little boy not taking candy? (*He laughed, putting a handful into a bag and handing it to the boy.*)
MOTHER (*when they were outside*): Why didn't you take the candy yourself?
LITTLE BOY: His hand is bigger than mine.

Q: What has a head, a tail, four legs, and sees equally well from both ends?
A: A blind mule.

"*I wove this basket myself,*" *he said craftily.*

"Be careful with that knife!" Tom said cuttingly.

"*Fortunately I like Chinese cookies,*" *said Tom.*

"I'll take two hot dogs," said Tom frankly.

"*I just completed orbit twenty,*" *he said dizzily.*

"Hand me the vial," said the chemist acidly.

"*I sing tenor in the chorus,*" *said Tom gleefully.*

Confucius say, "Many men smoke, but Fu Manchu."

Q: What would happen if cows were put in orbit?
A: It would be the first herd shot around the world!

SHE: *Why do dragons go to sleep in the daytime?*
HE: *So they can hunt knights.*

FIRST CLASS: How do you make a bedroll?
SECOND CLASS: Push it!

From the editors and writers of Boy's LIFE magazine, here are three new books for young people who "do things," including Cub Scouts:

Fun With Nature Hobbies
By William Hillcourt (Green Bar Bill)

Bird Feeders and Shelters You Can Make
by Ted S. Pettit

The Cub Book
by Dick Wingert

© Boy Scouts of America

You may also chuckle over

Jokes and How to Tell Them
by Sonny Fox

Funnier Than the First One
by Sonny Fox

Syd Hoff's Joke Book
by Syd Hoff